MAINSTREAM NEWS

Published in the United States of America by Cherry Lake Publishing
Ann Arbor, Michigan
www.cherrylakepublishing.com

Content Adviser: Jessica Haag, MA, Communication and Media Studies
Reading Adviser: Cecilia Minden, PhD, Literacy expert and children's author

Photo Credits: ©IxMaster/Shutterstock.com, Cover, 1; ©Everett Collection/Shutterstock.com, 5; ©sirtravelalot/
Shutterstock.com, 6; ©Anton_Ivanov/Shutterstock.com, 7; ©Sergei Kolesnikov/Shutterstock.com, 8;
Commercial advertisement for radio station WWJ in Detroit, Michigan/Public Domain/Wikimedia
Commons, 9; ©Rawpixel.com/Shutterstock.com, 10; ©Images By Kenny/Shutterstock.com, 13; ©2p2play/
Shutterstock.com, 14; ©Yulia Reznikov/Shutterstock.com, 15; ©0meer/Shutterstock.com, 16; ©Mark Van
Scyoc/Shutterstock.com, 19; ©Morrowind/Shutterstock.com, 20; Federal Communications Commission/
Public Domain/flickr.com, 21; ©Anton Gvozdikov/Shutterstock.com, 22; ©aradaphotography/Shutterstock.com, 25;
©S_Jittisak/Shutt restock.com, 26; ©nelen/Shutterstock.com, 27; ©Africa Studio/Shutterstock.com, 28

Library of Congress Cataloging-in-Publication Data

Names: Mara, Wil, author.
Title: Mainstream news / by Wil Mara.
Description: Ann Arbor : Cherry Lake Publishing, [2018] | Series: Global citizens: modern media |
    Includes bibliographical references and index.
Identifiers: LCCN 2018005238 | ISBN 9781534129313 (hardcover) | ISBN 9781534131019 (pdf) |
    ISBN 9781534132511 (pbk.) | ISBN 9781534134218 (hosted ebook)
Subjects: LCSH: Journalism—Juvenile literature. | Mass media—Juvenile literature.
Classification: LCC PN4731 .M343 2018 | DDC 070.4—dc23
LC record available at https://lccn.loc.gov/2018005238

Cherry Lake Publishing would like to acknowledge the work of the Partnership for 21st Century Learning.
Please visit www.p21.org for more information.

Printed in the United States of America
Corporate Graphics

ABOUT THE AUTHOR

Wil Mara has been an author for over 30 years and has written more than 100 educational titles
for children. His books have been translated into more than a dozen languages and won numerous
awards. He also sits on the executive committee for the New Jersey affiliate of the United States
Library of Congress. You can find out more about Wil and his work at www.wilmara.com.

TABLE OF CONTENTS

CHAPTER 1

History: Popular News

People have been communicating with each other for thousands of years. What began as rock carvings has slowly changed into books, newspapers, magazines, movies, radio, TV, and the Internet. Together, they are called **media**.

The main purpose of media is to share news information. **Mainstream news** is the term that describes the largest, most widespread, and perhaps most influential delivery of that news. Mainstream news organizations report and often analyze events as they unfold. They usually have more money, more employees, and more locations than smaller, **alternative news** outlets.

During the early 20th century, paperboys and newsboys were young people distributing and selling newspapers.

Early Times

People have been delivering news to large segments of the population for centuries. The invention of the **printing press** in the mid-1400s helped make this happen. The press made it possible to distribute information to more people through pamphlets, flyers, posters, and newspapers. The first use of the word *newspaper* can be traced back to the 1500s. That's when the first newspapers were being printed in Germany.

Most newspapers today are printed using an offset printing press.

Rapid Growth

By the early 1800s, most of the Western world had regular newspapers. In 1805, the London newspaper *The Times* was producing more than 1,000 copies per hour! The first half of the 20th century saw massive growth in the newspaper business. With thousands of different newspapers around the globe, print media was the main way that most people got their news.

Electronic outlets soon began entering the field. Radio made its debut in news **broadcasting** in August 1920 in Detroit, Michigan,

Reading the newspaper was an easy and affordable way to stay updated on current events.

People have been tuning in to the radio for the news since the 1920s.

on station 8MK. Twenty years later, television entered the market, providing further competition with newspapers.

Television and Radio News

The first-ever regular television news program was broadcast by NBC in 1940. The American public took an even greater interest in radio and television reports following the attack on Pearl Harbor on December 7, 1941. And by the end of World War II in 1945, many stations expanded their news-oriented schedules to meet public demand.

[21ST CENTURY SKILLS LIBRARY]

Some sources indicate that when 8MK first broadcast
at least 30 homes in Detroit listened in.

Today, there are many ways to stay updated, from YouTube videos to posts on Facebook.

The Modern Era

The rest of the 20th century saw the growth of many mainstream news outlets. But the dawn of the 21st century saw the rise of something new: the **mergers** of media organizations. Large outlets, like Time Warner and America Online (AOL), began combining their resources to reach a larger audience. These mergers led to less competition, which led to the disappearance of smaller media outlets. In 1983, about 90 percent of the news media in the United States was controlled by roughly 50 different companies. Today, there are only six companies!

People also look to social media for news. About 67 percent of Americans get their news this way—and it's not just young people. According to a study, an estimated 55 percent of people age 50 and older use it to get updated on current events. Facebook, YouTube, and Twitter are the top social media platforms people go to for the news.

Developing Questions

Throughout history, the way in which people receive the news has changed. More people use social media to stay updated on current events. How do you think this changes the news industry?

CHAPTER 2

Geography: Mainstream News Around the World

Mainstream news is a part of daily life and even reported around the clock in the majority of countries. In the United States, a person can wake up and turn on CNN or MSNBC and learn about the major happenings of the day. The journalists who write these stories are generally free to research and report their findings.

But in some countries, there isn't the same degree of freedom for broadcasters or journalists. In nations where **free speech** is not a right, news content can be tightly **censored**. It is an ongoing challenge in those countries.

BREAKING NEWS

REAKING NEWS   CRITICISM GROWS OVER TRADE DEAL

IVE NEWS   drops ahead of policy meeting • Alliances under p

News stations around the world sometimes interrupt programs
to inform the public of breaking news.

Best Countries for Journalistic Freedom

Reporters Without Borders is a free-speech organization.
In 2017, it found that Western countries, like the United States,
England, Australia, and Norway, enjoy a high amount of journalistic
freedom and independence. In the United States, free speech and
freedom of the press are protected by the First Amendment to the
Constitution. England, Australia, and Norway have similar
protections as well.

An investigative reporter researches and reports on a single topic, like political corruption. Many countries don't like these types of reporters.

And the Worst...

Journalism can be a very dangerous profession in countries where free speech is not a right. Countries like North Korea and Saudi Arabia have some of the strictest media regulations. In 2016, more than 250 journalists were jailed and nearly 80 died—all for reporting something the government did not agree with. In Mexico, there were over 425 reported attacks on journalists. In Turkey, more than 150 reporters have been jailed for writing negative articles about the president and the administration.

A list compiled by the Committee to Protect Journalists revealed that in 2015 China and Eritrea were the top countries that censor the news.

According to a 2017 U.S. report, local news reaches 18 percent more adults than national news.

The People in Control

There was a time when media outlets were owned by a small local company or even a family based in the same city. Regulations limited the number of media outlets those owners could have. This helped keep news reports more **objective** and balanced. In recent years, these conditions have drastically changed. Mainstream news outlets have become the property of large and powerful companies. These media mergers can limit competition and the types of stories produced.

The concentration of ownership isn't limited to the United States. It affects countries around the world. For instance, Australian-born Keith Rupert Murdoch owns or is on the **board of directors** of over 20 media outlets around the world! This type of control over the media is powerful. It could lead to a lack of **diverse** views and information. It also could influence the public's opinion over important matters, like presidential elections.

Gathering and Evaluating Sources

According to a study, Americans tend to trust their local news more than the national news. Only 38 percent of the people surveyed said they trusted national news sources more than their local news. Why do you think this is? Make a list of local news sources in your city. Make another list of national news sources in the United States. Does one news source seem more reliable? Why or why not? First find articles on the same subject from both a local and a national news source. Compare them. Then use the information you find to support your answer.

CHAPTER 3

Civics: Mainstream News and the Public

Mainstream news keeps us connected and updated on things happening across the world. With over 32,000 television and radio stations in the United States and social media at our fingertips, we are never without an update. Most journalists believe it is their duty to fairly and accurately report the news. But some argue that these news updates aren't as diverse or **unbiased** as they appear.

Rules and Regulations

One of the chief complaints about mainstream news is that it does not offer much in the way of diverse reporting. Today, there are six companies—General Electric, News Corp, CBS,

The FCC was established in 1934 when Congress passed the Communications Act.

Time Warner, Viacom, and Disney—that control about 90 percent of what people listen to, read, and watch. For instance, News Corp owns the *Wall Street Journal*, *The Sun*, and *The Australian*. These are the top newspapers in the United States, the United Kingdom, and Australia! And that's only three of News Corp's media outlets.

In the 1970s, the **Federal Communications Commission** (FCC) put regulations in place. These helped ensure healthy competition and diversity of thought in media outlets. In late

According to a 2017 study, about 48 percent of children say that watching and reading the news is important.

The FCC consists of five people who are chosen by the president.

2017, the regulations were abolished. This made it easier for more television and radio stations, magazines, and newspapers to be owned by fewer people and organizations. According to FCC Chairman Ajit Pai, the regulations were ended because of the growing use of the Internet. There are plenty of ways for people to get the news—like blogs, alternative news sites, podcasts, and social media. Critics, however, believe there is still a need for these regulations. They are afraid that mass media, including mainstream media, can become a **monopoly**.

As of 2013, only about 7 percent of reporters claimed they were conservatives. Why do you think this is?

Industry Location

There was a time when the mainstream news industry presented the views and feelings of both **conservatives** and **liberals**. Some argue this is no longer true. They believe more mainstream news sources tend to be liberal. The reason for this might be location-based, even though mainstream media jobs are available all around the country. In 2008, about 60 percent of the popular newspaper and online publishing jobs were in areas populated mostly by liberal voters. Only about 40 percent of those jobs could be found in conservative parts of the country. By 2016, those numbers widened even more. About 75 percent of media jobs were located in liberal areas, and only 25 percent were in conservative areas.

Developing Claims and Using Evidence

Objective news reporting should be the norm. Yet it often isn't. Read through your local newspaper and a mainstream news site. See how many articles you can find that are unbiased. Compare this to the number of articles you find that seem biased. What elements in an article make it objective? What elements make it **subjective**? *Use the evidence you find in the articles to support your claims.*

Economics: What the Numbers Tell Us

Mainstream news outlets earn a lot of money. But how does the financial factor affect the content of journalism? And what do the numbers tell us about the future of mainstream news?

The Trump Factor

President Donald Trump will likely go down in history as one of the most **controversial** figures of our time. In the news industry, this has translated into big money. For example, from May 2016 to May 2017, the cable-news station MSNBC enjoyed a jump in its **advertising revenue** of nearly 50 percent.

Bezos - Forbes

Tweet 199   in Share

22

THE SLOW COLLECTION

#1

+ Follow Bezos

Real Time Ne

$34.2

CEO and Founon.com

Age

Amazon.com, S
Ma

Source Of Weal

Seattle,

Self-Made

United Sta

Jeff Bezos, founder of Amazon.com, owns the *Washington Post*.
It only cost him $250 million!

The more emotional or controversial a news story is,
the more people tend to tune in.

The reason for this was because more people were watching its
reports about Donald Trump. CNN experienced a similar rise in
ad revenue during the same time. Stories that make people happy
or angry can mean big money for mainstream news outlets.

Putting Their Money Elsewhere

If a company wishes to advertise its products or services, it
spends money on advertisements. For a long time, most of those
advertising dollars were spent for ads on television and in print

About 76 percent of teenagers get their news from social media sites.

Only about 5 percent of 18- to 29-year-olds get their news from newspapers.

media. But as the Internet grew, many of those ad dollars headed online. Traditional forms of media started seeing ad revenues drop.

Taking Informed Action

Mainstream news outlets have come under fire for being politically biased in their reporting. But not every alternative news outlet is innocent either. Try to find the most trustworthy news outlets. Compile a list of outlets that appear to have good reputations for objective reporting. Why do you think these news sources are objective? Use evidence you've found to support your reasons.

In 2007, for example, companies around the world spent about 40 percent of their advertising budgets on newspaper and magazine ads. Digital media outlets represented only about 10 percent of the ad budget. Ten years later, those numbers flipped. Fifteen percent of the budget was spent on ads in print media, and 33 percent was spent on online ads. The only place that has stayed relatively the same is television. Television has seen fairly steady ad revenues in the 21st century.

Communicating Conclusions

Before reading this book, did you know about mainstream news? Now that you know more, why do you think it's important to learn about the industry? Many people have strong opinions about news sources that they believe to be reliable and unbiased. What do you think about mainstream news? What about alternative news sources? Ask your friends and family what they think about mainstream news and alternative news sources. Discuss the advantages and disadvantages of both types of news.

Think About It

More adults are turning to the Internet for news than ever before. And they're doing it on their mobile devices, like smartphones and tablets. In 2017, 45 percent of all adults said they frequently used a mobile device to get their news. A year earlier, this number was only 36 percent. In 2013, only 21 percent of American adults said they used a mobile device to read the news. This means that in just 4 years, the percent of American adults getting their news through smartphones or tablets more than doubled! What does this data tell you about the future of mainstream news? What do you think this means for the more traditional media outlets, like television, newspapers, and magazines?

For More Information

Further Reading

Heitner, Devorah. *Screenwise: Helping Kids Thrive (and Survive) in Their Digital World.* Brookline, MA: Bibliomotion, Inc., 2016.

Mahoney, Ellen Voelckers. *Nellie Bly and Investigative Journalism for Kids: Mighty Muckrakers from the Golden Age to Today, with 21 Activities.* Chicago: Chicago Review Press, 2015.

Mooney, Carla. *Asking Questions About How the News Is Created.* Ann Arbor, MI: Cherry Lake Publishing, 2016.

Websites

Smithsonian—TweenTribune
www.tweentribune.com
Visit this daily news site for young people.

Youngzine
youngzine.org
Learn about current events around the world.

GLOSSARY

advertising revenue (AD-vur-tize-ing REV-uh-noo) money made by a media outlet from companies that want to promote products and services through them

alternative news (awl-TUR-nuh-tiv NOOZ) news that is separate and apart from mainstream news, reflecting less common views

board of directors (BORD UHV duh-REK-turz) a group of people who manage or direct a company or organization

broadcasting (BRAWD-kast-ing) delivering a program to an audience by radio or television

censored (SEN-surd) kept certain news items from being published

conservatives (kuhn-SUR-vuh-tivz) people who tend to value and maintain existing or traditional order; often referred to as the right or right wing

controversial (kahn-truh-VUR-shuhl) causing a great deal of disagreement

diverse (dih-VURS) having many different types of kinds of something; varied

Federal Communications Commission (FED-ur-uhl kuh-myoo-nih-KAY-shunz kuh-MISH-uhn) a government agency in the United States that regulates radio, television, wire, satellite, and cable

free speech (FREE SPEECH) the right to speak, write, or otherwise communicate freely about what is on your mind

liberals (LIB-ur-uhlz) people who are in favor of political progress; often referred to as the left or left wing

mainstream news (MAYN-streem NOOZ) refers to the various large and popular mass news media

media (ME-dee-uh) a method of communication between people, such as a newspaper

mergers (MUR-jurz) the joining of two businesses into one

monopoly (muh-NAH-puh-lee) a company that has the complete control of the supply of a service or product

objective (uhb-JEK-tiv) reporting a news story in a way that is not affected by the journalist's personal views

printing press (PRINT-ing PRES) a device designed to print ink onto paper in large quantities

subjective (suhb-JEK-tiv) reporting in a way that reflects the personal views of the journalist

unbiased (un-BYE-uhsd) not favoring or opposing a particular person or group

INDEX